cats

in their | gardens

Page Dickey

STEWART, TABORI & CHANG

New York

Text and photographs copyright © 2002 Page Dickey
Photographs of Rocky and Dela courtesy Hitch Lyman.

Published by
Stewart, Tabori & Chang
A Company of La Martinière Groupe
115 West 18th Street
New York, NY 10011

Export Sales to all countries except Canada, France,
and French-speaking Switzerland:
Thames and Hudson Ltd.
181A High Holborn
London WC1V 7QX
England

Canadian Distribution:
Canadian Manda Group
One Atlantic Avenue, Suite 105
Toronto, Ontario M6K 3E7
Canada

Library of Congress Cataloging-in-Publications Data
Dickey, Page.
    Cats in their gardens / Page Dickey
       p.cm.
    ISBN 1-58479-160-8
1. Cats—United States. 2. Cats—Europe. 3. Cats—United States—
Pictorial works. 4.
Cats—Europe—Pictorial works. 5. Gardens—United States. 6.
Gardens—Europe. 7.
Gardens—United States—Pictorial works. 8. Gardens—Europe—
Pictorial works. I. Title

SF445.5 .D54 2002
636.8—dc21   2002021171

Front cover: Ralph asleep on Cathy Croft's garden wall.
Page 1: Delaware & Western, known as Dela, Hitch Lyman's tomcat
named after an old train line, with purple colchicums.
Title page: Ralph with nasturtiums in Cathy Croft's New York garden.
Dedication: Asters and a kitten at Duck Hill.
Table of Contents: (clockwise, from top left) Gray Gatto asleep in
Barbara Talbot's flower garden in Connecticut; Cleo with black-eyed
Susans; Cathy Croft's Ralph among nasturtiums; Beluga in front of a
vase of helichrysums; Lewis in James David and Gary Peese's Texas
vegetable garden.
Introduction: Hitch Lyman's cat, Rock Island, known as Rocky, resting
in front of white colchicums.
Page 96: Ed Merrin's kitten under a hosta.
Back cover: (top) Bartok and Berlioz in Martha Stewarts' garden;
(bottom) Cleo with petunias at Duck Hill.

The text of this book was composed in Humanist typeface.

Printed in Singapore
10 9 8 7 6 5 4 3 2 1
First Printing

My thanks go first to all the cat owners
and gardeners in the book for their generous
cooperation—Larry Ashmead, Gene Bertrand,
Frank and Anne Cabot, John Coke, Cathy Croft,
James David, Keith and Alison Dickey, Marcia
Donahue, Joe Eck, Alexandra and Laura Fisher,
Carol Goldberg, Allen Haskell, Lois Himes,
Penelope Hobhouse, Ron Lutsko, Hitch Lyman,
Tovah Martin, Pepe and John Maynard, Ed
Merrin, Jeff and Janet Morris, Fred and Mary Ann
McGourty, Julie McIntyre, Gary Peese, Fred
Roberts, Barbara and Charles Robinson, Roxana
Robinson, Bob Scanzaroli, Martha Stewart,
Barbara, Peter, and William Talbot, Sam and Bitsy
Tatnall, Judy Tomkins, Wayne Winterrowd, Chris
Woods, and Robin Zitter.

This small book is in large part due to the
confidence of Janis Donnaud, Leslie Stoker,
Sandy Gilbert, and Elaine Schiebel, as well as the
skill of Miranda Ottewell—and the creativity of
Alexandra Maldonado—thank you all. Final
appreciation goes to my husband Bosco Schell
who is my collaborator in books as well as in life.

For my granddaughter Claire

8   INTRODUCTION

PROFILES

10   Duck Hill Denizens

14   Domain of Doubtless

20   High Life at the Tatnalls

22   Nasturtium Cats

28   Ocis on the Rocks

32   Sharing Marcia's World

38   Farm Cats

42   Cat in the Cannas

44   Maine Coons in Vermont

50   Hunting Grounds at
       Hillside Gardens

table of contents

54   California Calico

56   Himalayan Haven at Martha's

62   Alexandra's Pal

66   Texas Tom

72   Pest Control at Longwood

74   Topiary Keepers

76   Wig Wig in Dorset

82   Korat at Bury Court

86   Chanticleer Cat

90   Monk-Monk among the
        Flowerpots

VIGNETTES

18   Pusses in Poses

26   Up a Tree

36   "When in Doubt, Wash"

48   Cool Cats

60   Entente Cordiale

70   Cat Naps

80   Kitten Klatch

94   Cattails

introduction

Not long ago my husband and I were visiting
Gravetye Manor in England, once the home
of William Robinson, the Edwardian who is
considered the father of modern flower
gardening. As we set out on paths
through perennial borders and meadow
carpeted with cyclamens, we realized
that a small tabby cat was following us.
Soon she was beside us, or scampering
ahead as we wandered on, finally entering
Robinson's vast walled vegetable garden through a
wooden gate. That little cat gave life to the old garden with her spontaneity and charm.

Gardeners who are not cat lovers seem astonished at the notion that cats are satisfying, indeed delightful, companions in the garden. Many of us, however, would
not dream of having a garden that was not enlivened by cats as well as dogs, and a
notable number of gardeners actually choose the company of cats alone. English
author Beverly Nichols writes: "A garden without cats…can scarcely deserve to be
called a garden at all." Gertrude Jekyll, the great English gardener and writer, lived
alone at Munstead Wood in Sussex, England, contentedly sharing her days "inside and
out" with several tabbies. In 1908, she wrote a charming book, *Children and Gardens,*
in which a chapter is devoted to the delights of cats in the garden. "My garden would
not be half the pleasure it is to me without the pussies," she writes. "They are perfect garden companions. When I am out at work there is sure to be one or other of

them close by, lying on my jacket or on a bench if there is one near." Sidney Eddison, daylily expert and author, today reminisces about gardening in Connecticut with her cat Nigel: "When I was kneeling, which is my preferred way of gardening, he would lie across the calves of my legs. This kept him off the wet grass, and it was rather nice for it kept me warm."

Having gardened all my life with dogs and cats, I realize that cats give pleasure in a different way. They are a more benign presence in the garden. Independent and self-sufficient, they will not sit on command or stay or do anything, for that matter, they don't want to do; but neither do they dig, or bark, or trample the flowers. Although most cats are excellent hunters, culling the population of moles, voles, and mice that wreak havoc in our borders, they are often content to spend hours stretched out in the sun, baking in the heat of the pea gravel, draped languorously on a stone wall, or sprawled in the cool grass. I think the sensual pleasures of the garden particularly appeal to cats—the scents, the heat, the jungle atmosphere of massed flowers and grasses.

Like dogs, cats often add comic relief to the garden scene as they stalk grasshoppers and beetles and leap into the air after moths and dragonflies. Paul Gallico, in *Honorable Cat,* writes that "a cat's comedy is unconscious, slightly rueful, and often delicate." On the other hand, he adds, they are vain enough to "put themselves into positions that they know are admirable." In fact, cats are often showoffs, willing to strike attitudes for an audience, sitting, rolling, washing, yawning— always choosing the most becoming flowers or foliage in our gardens for background.

The following pages show how admirably a variety of cats inhabit some special gardens in America and abroad.

duck hill

DENIZENS

▲ Our young tom Felix meditates in the herb garden. Fragrant cottage pinks (_Dianthus plumarius_) are in flower. The terrace wall and steps leading into the nasturtium garden, seen here in June, are a favorite resting place.

Cleo, a calico, and black-and-white Felix are the resident cats at Duck Hill these days. Cleo arrived ten years ago, less than two months old, abandoned on a front stoop in Queens and brought here by kindly rescuers who had heard through the cat grapevine that I was looking for a calico kitten. Tiny, dainty, and spirited, she immediately set about chasing butterflies in the garden as though she had always done it. Felix is a recent adoption, not a foundling but born into a loving family in Brooklyn. Grandmother, parents, and two children came to check us out, making sure we were suitable owners for their adored kitten. Felix succeeds our old tabby Tom, and like him has grown into a lazy, lovable, oversize fellow. Although Felix and Cleo prefer to sleep all day and prowl at night, in spring, summer, and fall they do their daytime lounging with us in the garden. Our young dogs, Noodle and Roux, who like to run, chase, and bark during the day, are something of a

▲ Cleo, the calico, seems to know that black-eyed Susans are particularly becoming to her. Felix checks out a weeding basket on the terrace before settling down to chew some catmint.

trial for the dozing cats. But Cleo and Felix have the patience the pups lack, and sooner or later the dogs get bored and go off to find amusement elsewhere, leaving the cats to resume their naps in peace.

Their preferred spot for lounging is the gravel terrace just outside our kitchen doors. The terrace is bound by low stone retaining walls; steps lead up to a herb garden in the center and, on one side, to what we call the nasturtium garden because of its color scheme, in warm hues ranging from red to yellow. Whereas the dogs are more apt to lie on the soft thyme-blanketed paths of the herb garden on a spring or summer day, the pusses love the sun-baked feel of the stone. They roll in the gravel, back legs and tail extended, white stomachs exposed, then move to the wall for a wash and a snooze. Walls are not only warm from the sun, but good vantage points from which to keep tabs on gardeners and mischievous dogs.

The terrace and paths leading through the gardens

above are covered with a thin layer of unwashed pea gravel, which turns out to be a great medium for growing things. Catmint, originally underplanting roses along the wall, leaped over the brick edging and seeded itself in the gravel. Johnny-jump-ups followed suit, and corydalis, a lovely white form given to me by a friend. Alliums have since appeared in the gravel as well as patches of vibrant blue scilla. A delicate cream-colored scabiosa threatens to take over, and by the kitchen, spearmint worms its way through the gravel, sending up wafts of refreshing perfume as we tread on it.

Visitors with a strong sense of neatness might be disturbed by the apparent disorder of the terrace gravel garden, but the cats love it. The pungent catmint is good to roll in, equally good to chew; an occasional towering mullein makes a fine umbrella; and any sort of jungly growth is to their liking, serving as hiding places if they choose or, more likely, dramatically framing their poses.

DOMAIN
of doubtless

The entrance to author Roxana Robinson's Victorian house is charmingly secretive. Having parked your car in the gravel under the old willow tree, you head for a high wooden gate in the white-painted board fence that separates the house and garden from the drive. Gates are by nature alluring, with their suggestion of an adventure on the other side, but Roxana's gate is given a particular appeal by its whimsical design. Fat balls top the posts, and the solid board gate is cut in an arch and pierced in two delicate swoops. Pushing it open, you find yourself in Roxana's back garden, where brick paths leading to the kitchen, the porch, and a gazebo have the same playful,

swirling character as the gate. A stone wall, dripping with catmint, corydalis, and pinks, surrounds the area, dividing and sheltering it from higher ground that leads to meadow and orchard. At the foot of the wall, Roxana fills narrow borders with old-fashioned perennials and shrubs— peonies, campanulas, astilbes, cranesbills, lilies, scented roses—edging them with lamb's ears where the sun is strong, and hostas where there's shade. Outside the kitchen door, lettuces and culinary herbs mingle in beds with roses and catmint and bushes of box.

If she is not up in her studio writing another novel, you will find Roxana in this very private part of her garden, tending her flowers. Lacy, her standard poodle, and Doubtless, her twenty-year-old tabby cat, will be with her. Many cats have shared the house and garden with Roxana and her husband Tony over the years, but Doubtless is the

▲ Roxana Robinson's tabby, Doubtless, is alert but a little wobbly at twenty years old. He pauses in front of the garden gate, flanked by lamb's ears, boxwood, and a blooming 'Mary Rose' on a morning in late May.

▲ Brick paths run in pleasing curves from the gate to the doors of the house. Doubtless, along with Lacy the poodle, keep Roxana company while she gardens.

sweetest, according to Roxana, and the funniest. Although now he is a little wobbly on his feet, in his heyday "he had a gift for making a comical statement in the landscape." When the Robinsons opened the bedroom shade in the morning, "there he was sitting in the crotch of the tree just outside our window, waiting to greet us." Or, as they walked to the meadow, he'd be "perched in a fur ball" on top of the split-rail fence post. "Other cats are all business," Roxana adds, "but Doubtless has a charming sense of humor." He is also very gentle, according to his mistress. "He hates fighting. The worst thing he'll do, if you're treating a tender cut for instance, is hit you with a soft paw."

Doubtless started out life precariously at a friend's country property. He was brought there by her gardener one weekend when the Robinsons happened to be visiting. The kitten was to take up residence in the garden's greenhouse. But the tiny fellow, lonely and fearless, kept

scampering off to the house—territory guarded by an
unfriendly German shepherd. At one point, the guests
noticed the shepherd stalking something. "He's after the
kitten, doubtless," one of them said. At their friend's urg-
ing, the Robinsons came to the rescue, took the kitten
home—and named him Doubtless.

◀ clockwise *Tito, Robin Zitter's old orange tabby, on a wooden seat built in some of the ledge rock that rises in the woodland behind her garden; Judy Tomkins' lithe red Abyssinian, Zoe, rests for a second, sphinxlike, outside the newly built porch; Felix on alert on the kitchen terrace, his tuxedo front in full view; graceful Buckwheat at the Tatnalls; Achilles, hamming for his audience in Joe Eck and Wayne Winterrowd's garden.*

pusses in poses

high life at
THE TATNALLS

Sam Tatnall, a computer software engineer, lovingly works many hours in his vegetable and flower garden an hour north of New York City. On weekends, he is joined by his wife Bitsy Field, when she's not decorating houses for city clients. But Sam's constant companions while he gardens are two tomcats. Pale apricot Barley is the alpha cat, a venerable presence now at age fourteen, his cabbage ear, notched and flopped forward, attesting to a former life of

caterwauling. It's part of his roguish charm, according to Bitsy. Buckwheat, a sleek white cat with startling blue eyes, is a more recent addition. "Word got out," Sam says, "that life at the Tatnall's was a dish of cream."

The young china-white cat walked down their driveway one cold winter day, unannounced, chilled, and thin from lack of food. Sam fed him and placed a box with a blanket on the front porch. But he still seemed so cold that Sam moved him into the closed garage and showed him how to use the cat-door flap to get outside. "Of course, he figured out how to use the cat door that gets into the house, and next thing we knew, he was settled inside. I said to Barley, 'How do you feel about him?' Barley took one look at him, shrugged his shoulders, and walked away."

In gratitude, perhaps, for having been taken in, Buckwheat is inseparable from Sam, following him everywhere, hissing at Bitsy if she intervenes. When Sam tends his vegetables and cutting flowers, Bucky's preferred position is draped across his shoulders. From here he has a good view of the proceedings, helped by his talent for swiveling his head almost all the way around. "He's like an omen cat," Bitsy says, "perhaps born in an egg."

◀ Buckwheat, Sam Tatnall's white cat, surveys the garden from the back porch. When there's gardening to be done, however, his preferred place is on Sam's shoulder. Barley, the alpha cat, shows off his roguish charm.

nasturtium
CATS

Eight years ago, a handsome black-and-white cat appeared on Cathy and Chris Croft's doorstep in North Salem, New York. The Croft's only son, Blake, had just left home for his first year of college; he says he's certain the cat was sent as his replacement. Cathy and Chris named him Ralph, but they find themselves sometimes referring to him as "the kid."

The Crofts and Ralph moved recently to a new home set high on a meadow in upstate country laced with picturesque reservoirs. Cathy, a talented florist and professional gardener, immediately set about building a new garden. With her husband's help, she terraced the land as it dropped away from the house, laid stone walls, threaded steps through the middle, and planted the tiers

▲ Ralph takes his afternoon nap on the garden wall. Ginger, the kitten, would prefer to play. She eyes the seedheads of

with a colorful mixture of summer-blooming perennials and annuals. She interspersed herbs nearest the house and added rhubarb and blueberries among the flowers and ornamental grasses for summer, autumn, and winter interest. Yellow and scarlet nasturtiums and wine-colored perilla now seed in the paths. Tender tropical plants—cannas, amaranths, and phygelius—are added yearly for bold splashes of foliage and color. Cathy's garden is completely organic—no chemicals threaten the bird life, butterflies, and pets she and her husband love.

Ralph now shares the garden with a young female puss named Ginger. She is also black and white in coloring, but

blackberry lilies (*Belamcanda chinensis*) spilling over the wall, which are almost as decorative as the irislike flowers that preceded them.

with some Maine coon cat in her breeding. As she matures, her hair is getting longer and tufts are developing at her cheeks. The two cats share a love of the outdoors and are excellent mousers. Ralph is "a man about town," Cathy says. Outgoing and friendly, he loves to greet people as they arrive. He checks out their cars and lifts his tail on their tires. Morning and night, he enjoys sitting in the field below their house, looking for action, but in the afternoon he sleeps in the garden. According to Cathy, the cats hate the winter. "Ralph gets cabin fever, and Ginger is depressed." By nature playful, and whimsical-looking with smudges of black on her white snout, Ginger is surprisingly clumsy. "She has lead feet," says Cathy, "which is too bad, because we named her after Ginger Rogers."

▲ Nasturtiums seed along the steps in Cathy Croft's garden. Ginger stalks among purple amaranths and chartreuse potato vines, some of the many tender tropicals Cathy plants in her upstate New York garden for summer pizzazz.

up a tree

▶ clockwise *Felix in an old ash tree, wondering how he'll get down; Felix feeling macho; Maine coon cat Achilles in the willow; Cleo hides from the dogs in the arbor; Felix, owl-like, above Helianthus 'Lemon Queen;' Felix does a trapeze act in the apple tree.*

OCIS
on the rocks

Two ocicats, Mocha and Cinnamon, lend an exotic air to
the exquisite woodland garden belonging to Pepe and
John Maynard. Named for the beautiful wild ocelot, ocicats have a similar appearance, their spotted coat colored
a rich red brown—"the color of a dried oak leaf," Pepe
says. A fairly new domestic breed developed in Michigan
in the 1960s, the ocicat owes its spotted coat pattern to
the unexpected result of a cross of three-quarters Siamese
and one-quarter Abyssinian. Later, American shorthairs
were introduced in the breeding to make the cat less lean
in body. Besides looking elegant, ocicats are amazingly
sociable, according to Pepe. The only other cat she has
owned, a Tonkanese called Twilight whom she adored but

▲ Mocha and Cinnamon, Pepe and John Maynard's ocicats, spend much of their time on the walls Pepe built to terrace her hillside garden. If you visit Pepe's serene and richly planted garden, the cats greet you at the front steps, where hydrangeas are staged in summer.

found quite aloof by comparison, was tragically run over a few years ago. "I buried her under one of my golden magnolias, which has since grown huge."

Mocha and Cinnamon are sisters, but they are not very fond of each other. In fact, they are exceedingly territorial, Pepe has discovered. Mocha keeps to the north side of the three-acre garden, while Cinnamon commands the south side. Pepe takes her two dogs, a sheltie and an Australian shepherd, for a walk in the woods every day, and one or other of the cats invariably joins them. "If I walk out the south gate of the garden, Cinnamon is sure to come. If I walk out the north gate, Mocha will be waiting," Pepe says.

Pepe and John carved a terraced garden out of the steep, rocky oak woodland that surrounds their Bedford, New York, property. A garden designer and knowledge-

able plantsman, Pepe introduced flowering trees, such as Asian dogwoods, franklinias, and magnolias, that would flourish under the high oak canopy, and filled curving beds with lush patterns of perennials, wildflowers, and bulbs. Over fifteen years the garden has developed into a show-case of mostly shade plants that will grow in the dry, ledge-strewn, acid soil of her deciduous woodland. Stone retaining walls and steps lead from one level to another, offering a sense of surprise. Massive pots standing on the walls and terraces afford opportunities to mix annuals in pleasing colors and textures. Of course, the ocicats enjoy posing on the walls themselves. They are a constant presence when Pepe works in the garden. "They like to be where you are," she says. "You know how most cats want everything on their own terms. Mocha and Cinnamon want to be part of the family, the social group." When Pepe and John's garden is open to the public, as it is at least twice a year, the cats are delighted. "They spend the whole day walking around talking to people."

▲ The two ocicats always want to be a part of the family, which includes the Maynards's two dogs, Poppy and Bluebell. Poppy, a red merle Australian shepherd, and Mocha wait for their mistress on one of the walks between garden borders.

sharing
MARCIA'S WORLD

Marcia Donahue is a stone carver and ceramic artist with a passion for garden plants. The garden she has created over the last twenty-three years is small—a mere sixty by one hundred feet—and surrounds her Victorian house in downtown Berkeley, California. It is a jungle of semitropical foliage and flowers, combined with an eye for patterns and colors, and interwoven with an imaginative, quirky collection of objects and artworks. A showcase for Marcia's artistry as well as the works of her friends, the garden serves as a gallery and is open to visitors every Sunday afternoon.

Through a wooden gate shaped like a hand, you enter a world where sinuous brick paths cut between plants layered in striking juxtapositions. Cypress shaped like corkscrews tower over tree ferns, phormiums, grasses,

▲ Mama, a long-haired calico, and Wink, a marmalade tom, share sculptor Marcia Donahue's exotic and quirky garden in Berkeley, California. A towering figure of a woman known as the Big Beauty greets you among oversize cannas and bamboos. Carved pillows of stones serve as resting stops for Mama as she leads the way around the garden paths.

abutilons, and salvias. Cobalt blue vodka bottles sprout from branches of a tall *Leptospermum ericoides* or top stems of bamboo, and silver gazing balls hang like giant Christmas ornaments from high limbs, together with metal spirals fashioned by Marcia's artist friend, Mark Bulwinkle. Stones carved in the shape of pillows with tassels ("tuffets," Marcia calls them), or etched with words or faces, rest quietly along the walks. Painted ceramic bamboo stalks thrust through exotic fronds; broken pottery chards and marbles mix with pebbles underfoot; forks and knives jammed into the earth delineate paths; and bowling balls serve as mulch under groves of bamboo and acanthus. Marcia started collecting the painted balls years ago, bringing them home from bowling alleys that were going out of business. "I had them on my mantel," she explained; "then, when I wanted to paint the living room, I put them out in the garden and thought, wow, how great they looked. They're such satisfying orbs."

Sharing this rich and curious world with Marcia and her visitors are two cats, Mama, an "ancient" long-haired calico, and Wink, a two-year-old orange tabby. "Mama arrived

barefoot and pregnant many years ago and wouldn't take no for an answer," Marcia says. She is cranky now in her old age, according to her mistress, but "when you're in her good graces, she does arabesques by extending her rear leg." She is apt to accompany you on a garden walk, her plumed tail waving to show the way; as you stop to examine the plantings, she will sit poised patiently on top of a curved stone ball, or pause to sip water from an oversize ceramic jar.

Marcia first spied Wink as a tiny kitten on the street eating garbage. He was half-wild and homeless. Well fed now, "Winky lives for love," Marcia says; "he's very devoted to me, and only skittish with strangers." Visitors to the garden catch sight of him disappearing around a curve in the brick path, peering through the grasses, or stalking among the palm fronds. Although no boundaries keep them in, the two cats don't wander, Marcia says. They recognize the garden as their haven.

▲ Each turn in Marcia's tiny garden reveals creative combinations of flowers and leaves as well as artifacts that startle and amuse. Ceramic snails climb up a post, stone acorns fall to the ground, and paths are littered with a colorful mix of marbles and broken china. Shy Wink peers out at visitors through a jungle of fronds and grasses.

"when in doubt, wash"

▲ clockwise *Ron Lutsko's
calico Kitsy preening in this California
garden of herbs and native bunchgrass;
Boris among the flowers on Allen Haskell's
Massachusetts terrace; Felix doing his
nails amid herbs at Duck Hill; Tito on the
terrace outside Robin Zitter's Connecticut
house; ocicat Cinnamon sunbathing in
Pepe Maynard's garden.*

farm CATS

Beluga, a black-and-white tom, and Mewsy, a tricolor (gray, white, and orange), no longer hang out in a stable full of hay, mice, and stamping horses. Instead, they spend their days in a cottage garden overflowing with color and fragrance.

Their mistress, Carol Goldberg, boarded horses in her barns for two decades. Her days were filled with teaching riders, training, and judging horse shows. Equestrians filled her driveway with cars, walked their horses on her lawn, and made it impossible for her to be outdoors with any privacy from dawn until dusk. One day she got fed up. Out went the horses, the riders, the stable help, the rooms full of saddles and bridles. Down came the newer of the two barns, the one she had built to house ten more stalls. In its place, in soil blessedly enriched with aged horse manure, she made a garden.

Carol came to gardening late, and accidentally. One year, when she was still busy training horses, she planted a

small border of heucheras, daylilies, and astilbes by the walk that led up to her Victorian farmhouse. The sight of it filled her with unexpected pleasure. Next she dug a bigger, deeper flower border along the south-facing wall of the horse barn, gradually extending it along the stone wall that divides her lawn from the field where the horses grazed. That satisfied her for a year or two. But she started dreaming of a more elaborate garden, one she could have if that second barn and all those horses were not there.

By leveling the barn, Carol gained a flat space in which to create a formally patterned garden in full view of her kitchen and terrace. She filled the beds with brightly

▲ Beluga spends his days among blue agastache, red hibiscus, and pink cleomes on ground where, not long ago, a barn stood. He has made the transition from barn cat to garden cat without missing a step.

▲ Mewsy, the young tri-color, and black Beluga keep their mistress, Carol Goldberg, company in her garden. Carol leveled a horse stable in order to create the cottage garden she colored perennials and annuals that caught her eye at the nurseries. Fat boxwoods were planted to frame the blowsy blooms; an old vase used to mark the garden's center, together with a wooden arbor made from old bedposts, provides focus year round. When she's not digging, pruning, and weeding, Carol sits on a lawn chair gazing at her garden, with no more company than two cats and an elderly Norfolk terrier.

Carol doesn't miss the horse business. Neither does Beluga or Mewsy. Four-year-old Mewsy moved from barn to house and garden without blinking, and according to Carol, follows her around like a dog. Seventeen-year-old

Beluga lived in the barn his whole life—until three years ago. "He's gone from sleeping in the hayloft to sleeping on my bed," Carol says, adding that it was an easy transition. "He's a real mush for a barn cat. If you're watching TV, he jumps in your lap, and, if you stop scratching him for a minute, he bats your face with his paw."

Like Mewsy, Beluga wandered into Carol's farm as a kitten. "I heard this racket at the window, and there he was, the size of a mouse, sitting on the sill, yowling. Somebody in the barn named him Beluga, thinking of the black-and-white whale. She was mixed up. He should have been named Orca."

dreamed of. An urn spilling helichrysums marks its center. In a gravel courtyard, an old pig cauldron is planted with chives, 'Stella d'Oro' daylilies, and golden plectranthus.

cat in the CANNAS

Barbara Paul Robinson spends her weekdays in New York City working as a high-powered lawyer. Her puss, C.C. (short for Calico Cat), whiles away the days in the apartment she shares with her husband Charles, an artist. But on weekends Barbara, Charles, and C.C. get in the car and drive up to their garden in northwestern Connecticut, where their hearts are. In 1971 Barbara and Charles bought the old farmhouse and property they call Brush Hill to use on weekends. Barbara was not a gardener in those days; but "I'm a tidier by nature," she says, "so I got busy tidying the outside as well as the inside."

At first they thought they would keep the grounds very

simple, requiring the minimum of upkeep. They innocently planted a small vegetable garden. "Well, you know, when the peas come in, you get very excited," Barbara recalls, explaining the start of her passion for gardening. "It's a disease," she says. "Forget low maintenance." Barbara even took a sabbatical from her law firm to intern at Rosemary Verey's renowned garden, Barnsley House, in England. Charles was smitten too, not with plants but with the bigger landscape—moving earth, building bridges, arbors, and follies, digging ponds and pools.

The garden that Barbara and Charles created, now embraces a rose walk, terraced herbaceous borders, and a planted woodland laced with paths and a series of cascading pools. Four-year-old C.C. has fields in which to stalk, an allée of catmint to roll in, daylilies and cannas to hide under, and stone walls for rousting out chipmunks and mice. On Sundays, it's back to the city, where C.C. rests and dreams of her life in the garden at Brush Hill.

▲ C.C., short for Calico Cat, spends her weeks in New York City and her weekends immersed in plant life at Barbara Robinson's northwestern Connecticut garden. When she's not stalking in the meadow, C.C. follows Barbara as she tends her colorful borders.

maine coons
IN VERMONT

Landscape designers Joe Eck and Wayne Winterrowd have shared their life at North Hill in rural Vermont with a series of pedigreed Maine coon cats for the last ten years. When asked how they would describe Maine coons as differing from other cats, their unhesitating reply is, "Affectionate independence." "We've had cats all our lives," Joe says, "and they were either aloof or overly attached, until we discovered Maine coon cats. These combine both traits—they're enormously affectionate but self-reliant. They'll come to be scratched for a while, then go off to sleep in a chair."

In residence at North Hill now are eight-year-old, silver-coated Helen and three of her grandchildren: Artemis, a bashful brown female with a lion face, and two outgoing toms, Achilles and Demetrius, both with silken pale gray fur. When not sprawled on the beds in Joe and

◀ Achilles stands in a bower of hydrangeas by the entrance to the pergola in Joe Eck and Wayne Winterrowd's delightful Vermont garden. Chestnut-striped Artemis looks out from yellow corydalis on the greenhouse wall.

▲ Tawny Artemis, here by the greenhouse windows, is bashful compared to her silver-coated brothers Achilles and Demetrius, lounging under the arbor. Joe holds Achilles, "a great bear of a cat" at twenty pounds. Maine

Wayne's cozy clapboard house, the cats are in the garden. They are not alone. Two collie dogs, a gaggle of strutting Sebastopol geese, fancy chickens, and Scottish Highland cattle are among the other furred and feathered denizens at North Hill.

Joe and Wayne's idyllic New England garden, known nationally because of their personal and informative book, *A Year at North Hill*, is their passion as well as the source of their livelihood. Its creation in the harsh climate of Vermont, and the knowledge gained from that experience, led Joe and Wayne to author books and magazine articles not only about their own garden but about plants and garden design in general. They now hold a symposium every June to present the brightest new garden designers and plantsmen to an enthusiastic public. A bonus is the opportunity to stroll leisurely through their garden.

For twenty-five years, the two men have worked to transform a five-acre south-facing slope in a wooded valley into the richly diverse garden they preside over today. Intimate terraces lead from the weathered wooden house to shrub, rose and perennial borders, lushly planted woods cut through by a stream, a vegetable garden, a rock garden, and a bog garden. Greenhouses full of exotic bulbs and tender flowering plants proffer cheer in the long winter months.

A good chunk of Joe and Wayne's days is spent writing, designing, and lecturing in distant places. But like so many gardeners who have gained some fame through their writings, they are most content when home at North Hill, working in the garden in the company of their beloved Maine coon cats. "We cannot go anywhere on the property," Joe says, "summer or winter, without the entire pride following us."

coons, America's native long-haired cats, Wayne says, "are sturdy, active, self-reliant, curious, intelligent, resourceful, and well insulated against the cold," excellent attributes for living in a northern New England garden.

▲ clockwise *Cinnamon, a spotted ocicat, drinks from the round lily pool just outside Pepe Maynard's bedroom door; Dusty Miller pauses for refreshment by the entrance steps to Fred and Mary Ann McGourty's garden; Wig Wig laps water from the square pool in the center of Penelope Hobhouse's walled garden in Dorset on a soft autumn day; Plucky-Lucky rests by the terrace reflection pool at Anne and Frank Cabot's Les Quatre Vents garden in Quebec; marmalade-striped Taz struts along the bluestone coping of Alexandra Fisher's swimming pool.*

cool cats

HUNTING *grounds*
AT HILLSIDE GARDENS

Two of the three cats who greet visitors at Fred and Mary Ann McGourty's renowned garden and nursery in Norfolk, Connecticut, are geriatric. Dusty Miller is a fourteen-year-old Russian blue mix, brought home as a kitten from the shelter. He was the alpha cat until he tangled with a moving car recently, and was left partially lame in his front legs. Dickens, a mackerel tabby, is nineteen, and a little slowed down by rheumatism. "He's the only cat in Norfolk on prednisone," Fred says. Blossom, a fluffy female Maine coon cat, is the baby at age eight, a Christmas present from Fred to Mary Ann.

The McGourtys' garden is a showplace as well as a testing ground for perennials suitable to their northeastern climate. Here, Fred and Mary Ann gather recently discovered cultivars, along with more ordinary sorts, and combine them brilliantly into tapestries of color and texture. They have had about thirty cats over the years to keep them company in the garden and help control the vermin—voles, chipmunks, and mice—that proliferate in the many dry stone

◀ Nineteen-year-old mackerel tabby, Dickens, passes Maine coon cat, Blossom, as she guards her territory in Fred and Mary Ann McGourty's renowned garden in Norfolk, Connecticut. Mary Ann cradles Blossom in front of borders of phloxes, snakeroots, sedums, and ornamental grasses.

▲ Dickens prefers to linger near the back terrace by the old stone water trough, where he gets Fred's attention. Blossom hides in the coreopsis.

walls that back their perennial borders and ribbon the property. Blossom, Dickens, and Dusty Miller are coaxed inside at five o'clock for dinner and kept in for the night because of coyotes. "They sleep in the cellar ever since Dickens deposited a mouse on Fred's pillow," Mary Ann says.

Each cat has a preferred territory in the garden. Dusty Miller lounges by the entrance steps and nursery, where he can readily greet visitors; Blossom stalks among the burnets, grasses, hostas, and snakeroots at the far edges of the garden; and Dickens basks near the terrace. The McGourtys have recently decided to cut back and close down their nursery. The cats rather resent it, according to Mary Ann: "They're people cats," happiest when the garden is bustling with friends and plant enthusiasts. "They're hams," Fred adds. "Dickens was so pleased when *The Victory Garden* came for a shoot, he licked the camera."

CALIFORNIA *calico*

"Do you notice how much cats like grasses?" landscape architect Ron Lutsko asked as we watched his calico Kitsy moving languorously through clumps of arching bunchgrass. "Perhaps they are transported back to their roots in the savannah," he mused. Young Kitsy paused to chew a blade among the native grasses and silvery herbs that blanket the dry slope above Ron's house. Ron lives in Lafayette, California, with Kitsy, his wife, Sandi, and two teenage daughters, and here he grows the plants he champions in his garden designs, species that flourish in the dry, mild climate of the area. Ron is passionate about the native flora of northern California, with its majestic oaks and picturesque manzanitas, its varied habitats of rock

outcroppings and raparian valleys; but he is not a purist. He creates gardens using his beloved natives together with plants from the Mediterranean coast, which has a similar climate, as well as from Australia and South Africa, that thrive in the region's hot, dry summers and mild, moist winters.

It was near a job site three hundred miles away that Ron found Kitsy. "I went to a phone booth, and this kitten jumped in my lap," he says. Realizing she was a stray, he decided to bring her home. He went to a diner, bought a tuna fish sandwich, and fed bits of it to her for the entire drive home. Not only beguiling in looks, with her patchwork coat of orange, gray, and white, but sweet-tempered, the kitten was embraced by his family and named Kitsy by the girls. She's "the best cat we've ever had," Ron says stoutly.

▲ Kitsy was brought home as a stray kitten by California landscape architect Ron Lutsko from a job site three hundred miles away. She adds a splash of color to Ron's dry hillside plantings of native bunchgrass and herbs like santolina and lavender.

himalayan
HAVEN
AT MARTHA'S

Seven Himalayan cats have the run of the garden at Martha Stewart's country home in Connecticut. They amble along the many paths that ribbon and crisscross through the cottage-style borders, their plumelike tails up with pleasure, their dark faces inscrutable, their attitudes gentle and friendly. Teenie and Weenie, the oldest at thirteen, are always with people, according to Martha's housekeeper Louisa Santos. The five others have musical names—brothers Berlioz and Bartok, Vivaldi and Verdi, and Mozart, a ten-year-old tom who is shy.

The Himalayan is a popular breed in America, the result of crosses between the Persian cat and the Siamese. It has the typical wide face, round eyes, and snub nose of the Persian, along with its short body and luxuriously thick, long hair. In coloring, however, the Himalayan reveals the

▲ Weenie, Bartok, and Berlioz are three of the seven Himalayan cats that live in Martha Stewart's charming Connecticut garden. Amiable, gentle cats, they loll in the grass along paths dividing the many borders, which are blowsy in summer, with relaxed clumps of perennials and annuals.

▲ The Himalayan breed, resulting from a cross between the Persian cat and the Siamese, is said to be livelier than the couch-potato Persian, but it retains the Persian's short body and silken long-haired coat. Its pattern of coloring is more like a Siamese, as illustrated here by tan-coated, chocolate-faced Bartok and cream-colored Weenie.

distinctive markings of the Siamese, a pale ground color with dark face, ears, legs, paws, and tail. In personality, Himalayans are said to be livelier than Persians, but less demanding, and certainly less vocal, than the Siamese. Martha's seven cats vary in coloring from Berlioz's palest cream with smoky points to the boldly cloaked charcoal and white of Vivaldi and Verdi, who look as though they had tangled somewhere along the way with an ordinary black-and-white patchwork puss.

This first garden of Martha's, to some extent familiar to us all from her early books and articles, is a charming example of an unpretentious New England cottage style, laid out in a pattern of beds threaded through with grass

paths, like so many old-time gardens of the Northeast. Its casual air gives it particular appeal; neither overly designed or rigidly planted, it is blowsy in late summer with a mixture of golden black-eyed Susans, fragrant phlox, willowy white and mauve-pink Japanese anemones, and fat disks of sedums. Peonies and poppies bloom earlier, along with airy thalictrums and fernlike astilbes. An occasional arch wound with vines casts shadows on the paths. Cranesbills, lungworts, coralbells, and lamb's ears hug the edges of the borders, and fuchsias and salvias drip touches of scarlet and true blue from above. It is a garden to lose oneself in, to while away the day, even if you're not a feline.

▲ Four-year-old Vivaldi lingers by the entrance to the garden, greeting visitors. Behind him, pink-flowering Japanese anemones billow over the gravel path on a September afternoon.

▲ clockwise *Our old tabby, Tom, doted on May, the Scottish deer-hound, seen here lying in the shade of the pine tree; Norfolk terrier pup Roux reconsiders chasing Felix who doesn't care; Plucky Lucky teases cairn terrier D'whinnie on the terrace steps of Frank and Anne Cabot's Quebec garden; Cleo bides her time until Noodle, our minia-ture dachshund, finds other amusement; Tom and May in the herb garden with Truff, my Jack Russell terrier.*

ALEXANDRA'S *pal*

Eighteen-year-old Alexandra Fisher brought a tiny marmalade tabby home from a local pet shop eighteen months ago and named him Taz. "I knew my mother would kill me," she says, but she also suspected she would get her way. "It took a lot of crying," Allie adds. Her mother, Laura, knowing that Allie would soon be off to college, was concerned about becoming the caretaker. But when she went into her daughter's room and saw the kitten, she was won over. "He was precious," she recalls, "so beautifully red and white, with big blue eyes."

Allie turns out to be a responsible cat owner, caring for Taz, feeding him, taking him to the vet. Laura says her daughter plays with her puss as though he were her child. In fact, Allie has a whole wardrobe of clothes for Taz, who patiently allows her to dress him up.

Unfettered by clothes while Allie's in school, Taz spends his days in the garden. He stalks flies, bees, and moths and romps around the boldly luxurious borders Laura has created. Just outside the porch of the old stone

◀ Alexandra Fisher's young red-and-white tabby, Taz, loves to play hide-and-seek in the boxwood parterres when his mistress is away at school. His daytime playground is the garden that Alexandra's mother, Laura, is developing with imaginative flair. Here, Allie greets Taz before he scampers off to hide behind the diving board.

▲ The topiary garden leading off the porch of the house, and the pergola by the pool, were designed as simple, bold architectural statements in the garden with the help of Laura's friend, designer Hitch Lyman. Taz explores them all.

house, designer Hitch Lyman created a topiary garden for Laura out of clipped boxwood. Taz adores the topiary, both Allie and Laura report, leaping in and out of the parterres, hiding in the shadow of a clipped spiral of box. "He's quite content to entertain himself in the garden all day," according to Laura. At dusk, concerned for his safety, Allie and Laura call him inside. "All I have to do is clap my hands and call his name, and he comes right away," Laura says. "He's like a dog," Allie adds, "except better trained. He knows all the tricks dogs know."

texas TOM

Lewis, according to James David and Gary Peese, is a fab-
ulous cat. "He's over the top," they say; and they should
know, for this handsome red-coated Abyssinian shares
their home and renowned garden in Austin, Texas. "A
number of our friends went out and got Abyssinians after
visiting here because they fell in love with Lewis," Gary
says. Described by the two men as at once gentle and

feisty, this highly intelligent cat is very playful—even now, at the age of ten. "This is not a lap cat," Gary adds, describing the typically energetic Abyssinian. Author Barbara Holland, in her excellent book *Secrets of the Cat*, concurs: "Going and lying down is what they don't do. If part of the purpose of other cats is to teach us the blessing of peacefulness, the lesson of the Aby is industry." Although at night Lewis is coaxed indoors, safe from marauding fox or coyote, he spends his days from morning until dusk keeping busy in James and Gary's two-acre southwestern stone and floral domain.

Landscape architect James deGrey David is known nationally for his bold, playful, inventive designs, so perfectly illustrated in his own garden. Here, on a steep hillside, limestone, granite, and gravel are used to brilliant effect, creating a series of linear walls, terraces, and steps,

◀ Ten-year-old Lewis, a red Abyssinian, shares his Austin, Texas, garden with its creators, James David and Gary Peese. All day long he patrols the two-acre domain, chasing away neighboring dogs and cats, prowling for snakes, and hunting mice. He lingers on the stone terraces carved into the hillside by James, a noted landscape architect.

▲ Lewis in the patterned vegetable garden, which is tended by Gary, a superb cook. At dusk, Lewis is coaxed indoors with the promise of dinner to be safe for the night from coyotes and fox; here he pauses for one last look.

as well as unexpected water features and quirky outbuildings, often with an appropriate Spanish air. An eclectic, imaginative mixture of plants, some native, others from Mexico and the Mediterranean, softens the stonework and intermingles in seemingly wild abandon. Dashes of color are suitably strong, on the house and in the flowers—red amaranths and cannas, orange cosmos, wild yellow zinnias, royal blue and velvety purple salvias—holding up to the glaring heat of a Texas summer.

Not only the place where James and Gary work and entertain, the garden is the testing ground for plants sold in the nursery and retail store the pair own and run. Gardens, as it is called, specializes in select plants that are suited to the central Texas climate. With its glamorous pots, hard-to-find seeds, plants, and bulbs, and seductive articles for the

home, it is the hopping place to shop in downtown Austin.

In their home and garden, as in the shop, every object, every pot, is especially chosen and artfully arranged by James and Gary. Even Lewis's food dish, a carved stone bowl set on a table outside the kitchen door, passes muster under James's discerning eye. Here Lewis eats his breakfast before following Gary down to the chicken house. "It's a daily routine," Gary says. "He'll even leave his food half finished if he sees me heading to feed the chickens. You see, there're mice down there." When Gary arrives, he shakes the door to the chicken house, and invariably a mouse or two will run out. "About once a week, Lewis catches one," Gary adds. Daily, Lewis chases neighboring cats and dogs, as well as snakes, out of the garden. At age ten, industry, indeed.

cat naps

▲ clockwise *Ocicat Mocha stretches to show her spots on Pepe Maynard's garden wall; Felix yawns in the midday heat; Teenie naps under the plant stand on Martha Stewart's front porch; Ralph doses in Cathy Croft's garden on a summer afternoon; Mocha snoozes in the sun.*

Natural Pest Control

The cats you see in the gardens are Longwood "employees" working in our integrated Pest Management Program. In return for maintaining a vigorous rodent patrol, they receive excellent pay and benefits. Each cat has a home in one of the shops located throughout the Gardens that they can access through their own pet door. They are fed regularly and receive routine medical care. Collars are not worn to prevent possible injuries.

Our cats are doing an important job; please do not distract them. They should not be handled, and because each has a distinct territory, they shouldn't be encouraged to follow you. If you see an injured cat, or one in the parking lot, please inform our Security staff.

pest control
AT LONGWOOD

Longwood Gardens, the extraordinary Pennsylvania horticultural display garden, developed in the early twentieth
century by Pierre du Pont and dedicated to the enjoyment
and education of the public, is at the forefront of organic
pest control. Their revolutionary "Pest Management
Program" can be described in one word: cats.

When director Fred Roberts came to Longwood in
1984, the garden was beset with rodents—mice, voles,
moles, and rabbits—playing havoc in the display beds. The
staff was using a traditional pesticide to combat the prob-
lem, a stomach poison that Fred worried was killing more
birds than rodents. Having grown up on a dairy farm where
cats were relied on to keep the rat population down, Fred
quickly banned the use of any virulent poison at Longwood
and instead brought in fifteen cats, spayed and vaccinated,

to patrol the gardens. Each cat keeps to his or her own territory in a specific garden, and is overseen by the gardeners of that particular area. Cat doors are evident in the adjacent potting sheds and greenhouses, where the hardworking hunters are fed and can bed down during the day in their nesting boxes. And the rodents are kept in check.

Noel, a sturdy gray-and-black-striped tabby, is the working cat in the Idea Garden. These five acres display a range of planting ideas for the home gardener—types of hedges, vines, groundcovers, roses, grasses, perennials. Noel patrols it alone, which is how she likes it, according to the *Longwood Chimes* newsletter. She used to work in the neighboring Hillside Garden, dividing the beat with two other cats, but she always had an affinity for the Idea Garden. As the *Chimes* reports, "She would often stroll over to check the place out, chat with the gardeners, and try to scare off the little Siamese twins Frankie and Paulie who were lucky enough to work there." After the Siamese cats were stolen a few years ago, Noel moved in. "Although she's got a lot of ground to cover and puts in long hours to keep up with all the work, she seems delighted with her new position."

▲ Noel, a striped tabby, is one of the employees at Longwood Gardens, the horticultural mecca in Pennsylvania. She is in charge of keeping the rodent population in check in her assigned territory, the five-acre Idea Garden, where planting ideas are displayed for the home gardener. Bob Scanzaroli, one of the three gardeners who tend this area, enjoys Noel's company.

topiary KEEPERS

▲ Long-haired, black-and-white Boris and The Monk, with his orange stripes, live at the home and nursery of Allen Haskell, known nation-wide for his plantsman's skills and his topiaries. The Monk

Allen Haskell is a garden designer with an exceptional eye for color. His orchestrations of flower and foliage hues are brilliantly conceived. It is his topiaries, however, that have made his nursery in New Bedford, Massachusetts, a mecca for gardeners all over the United States. Standard myrtles, rosemaries, silver-leaved teucrium, bold red gera-niums, and pink-flowered leptospermum, impeccably grown and clipped like lollipops, stand in row after row in long greenhouses. They are among the thousands of herbal topiaries Allen produces with his small staff and sells yearly. Smaller greenhouses shelter other tender pot plants—geraniums with patterned leaves, deeply colored streptocarpus, orchids, ivies, begonias. Outdoors, a collec-tion of carefully selected shrubs, trees, and perennials are

displayed in artful combinations in the garden areas that surround the nursery and extend to the eighteenth-century house Allen shares with his friend and business partner, Gene Bertrand.

Until you visit his place, you might not be aware of Allen's other enthusiasm—namely, furred and feathered creatures. Behind the nursery and garden rare breeds of hens and roosters strut in runs that extend from a row of chicken coops. By the nursery greenhouses, two cairn terriers greet you with leaps and tail wags. As you browse down the greenhouse aisles, you will catch sight of an old orange tabby named The Monk. "We call him the Greenhouse Cat," Allen says. "He is able to run down a bench from pot to pot without ever harming a twig."

Black-and-white Boris, a one-year-old, long-haired tom will more likely be found near Allen and Gene's house, gracing the brick terrace among coral fuchsias and plum-flowered geraniums. Rescued from a pet store, Boris refused to have anything to do with the nursery. "He wanted to live in the house and be with us," Allen says. "You know, I do a lot of shouting, but he just moved right in."

guards the greenhouses, where row upon row of herbal topiaries tempt the visitor. Boris is more apt to be found in Allen's eighteenth-century house, or on its brick terrace, dressed with furniture painted an unusual red-brown (Rust-Oleum paint primer) and potted fuchsias of a similar but brighter hue.

WIG WIG *in dorset*

▲ Wig Wig, Penelope Hobhouse's tomcat, on a November day in the secluded walled garden that opens off the new, red-painted garden room at the

Wig Wig, a marmalade tomcat, was dumped in the garden at Tintinhull along with his brother, a black kitten called Homer, according to writer and garden designer Penelope Hobhouse. That was thirteen years ago, when Penelope was living at this National Trust property in Somerset, England, tending and enhancing the glorious garden first laid out by Phyllis Reiss in the 1930s. "They were very thin and scraggly and took some time to adjust to comfort and love," Penelope recalls.

Eight years ago Penelope and her husband, John Malins, moved to Dorset, renovating an old carriage house to suit their needs and starting a garden from scratch—a prospect they found thrilling. Wig Wig and Homer came with them. It was quite a while before the two cats settled into their new home. Wig Wig is still very nervous, although he has taken to visitors since Homer died last year. Penelope describes him as "demanding and selfish at home. He has a complaining voice, which is used whenever he comes in."

back of the renovated carriage house. In late autumn, the yellow of euphorbias and gray of sages and cardoons contrast splendidly with the dark evergreen bones of the garden.

▲ The front of the house opens onto a serene expanse of lawn, bordered by hedges and pyramids of yew, and ending with a simple rectangular reflecting

Wig Wig happily spends much of his day outdoors, either in front of the house, where a hedge-lined sweep of lawn bleeds out into the breathtaking Dorset landscape of steeply rolling hills dotted with sheep, or in the very intimate walled garden behind the house. Here, in a light-filled half-acre enclosed by high brick walls just outside her garden room, Penelope established a formal framework of box bushes, yew pyramids, and tightly clipped robinia trees. Then she crisscrossed the ground with gravel paths and filled the beds with an informal explosion of perennials, herbs, annuals, and tender shrubs. A small square pool

edged in stone, now nicely mottled with lichens, marks the center of the garden. Following the paths, you can move from sunny open spaces, where purple variegated sage and euphorbias tumble into the paths, to dappled shade under the lacy robinias or arches of old species roses. As long as Penelope is working in the garden or visitors are strolling through it, Wig Wig will be around. "He is lonely now since Homer died," Penelope says; "but he is foul to other cats and dogs, so must remain alone." Perhaps he prefers to ornament Penelope Hobhouse's enchanting garden all by himself.

pool beneath a picturesque oak tree. Nothing disturbs your eye as it rises to the beautiful Dorset countryside, dotted with sheep, in the distance.

kitten klatch

▲ clockwise *A litter of kittens appeared from under the hostas in Ed Merrin's woodland garden, unexpected dividends from their supposedly spayed, mousing female; a basket of kittens in the autumn garden at Duck Hill; Crispin the Terrible peering out from the shrubbery in the garden of Jeff and Janet Morris; playtime at the Merrins'.*

korat at BURY COURT

▲ Plantsman John Coke walks in his autumn garden with his Korat cat, Zazou. John replaced the concrete yard of his farm in Surrey, England, with a garden designed by Dutch landscape

The small, slate-gray cat with a heart-shaped face and large, pale green eyes in John Coke's Surrey garden is a Korat. In its native Thailand, this ancient and pure breed has always been prized; Korats are considered to bring good fortune to their owners. Desmond Morris writes in his fascinating book *Cat World* that because of the symbolism of their coloring, Korats were used in rainmaking ceremonies: "They have sometimes been named the 'Cloud-colored Cat' and, because their eyes are the color

of young rice, they have been thought to help in producing a good crop."

Korats were never sold in their native land but were given as gifts, most usually to brides on their wedding day. In 1959 a pair of Korats was given to the American ambassador to Thailand; sent to America, they were the foundation of a breeding program. More Korats were obtained for breeding in the 1960s, but it wasn't until a decade later that the breed was established in England.

John says that Korats are "not at all nervous or high-strung." Zazou, his twelve-year old female, is a personable companion, riding on his shoulder or trotting after him in the walled garden. John, a knowledgeable plantsman, until last year ran one of England's most notable nurseries. He

architect Piet Oudolf. Cobbles were brought from Belgium to pave the paths, and perennials planted in naturalistic swaths. Artist Paul Anderson created a wooden sculpture for the pool as well as the bench where the cat awaits his master.

▲ Korats like Zazou are an ancient breed, prized in their native Thailand. They were thought to bring good fortune to their owners and were never sold, but given as gifts. Here Zazou hunts in the gravel and admires her reflection in the pool.

lives in the old sprawling farmhouse on his property, set deep in a valley of tree-lined pastures. When he moved here a few years ago, the farmyard square that his house embraces, and looks out onto, was all concrete. He removed the concrete and then asked a friend, the celebrated Dutch landscape architect Piet Oudolf, to design a garden. Around a central carpet of lawn punctuated by fat clipped yews, Piet planted great clumps of ornamental grasses (*Molinia* and *Deschampsia* species) to stand alone or weave through swaths of perennials. Paths were laid in bold patterns with cobbles from Belgium, and at one end of the yard, a striking sculpture made from old ship's oak

by Paul Anderson rises out of a large geometric pool.

John's is a contemporary garden in a venerable setting. The original farmyard walls of cream-colored stone and brick, now brightened by blue-painted doors and window frames, end in a series of old oasthouses, their cone-shaped roofs punctuating the sky. It seems a perfect place for an exotic cat of ancient lineage, dressed in a rather modern-looking mole-colored coat, to call her own.

CHANTICLEER cat

Visiting Chanticleer in Wayne, Pennsylvania, in late October, when this charmingly inventive garden is in its tawny autumn dress, you might be greeted by a buff-colored puss with a chocolate face, paws, and tail and startling blue eyes. This is Taylor, an eight-year-old female Siamese belonging to Julie McIntyre, a resident fellow at Chanticleer. Julie is involved in a two-year program, funded by the garden, to gain experience in the management practices of public horticulture; she is researching ways for botanical gardens to be more involved in conservation.

While Julie's working in her office, Taylor is busy welcoming visitors—on her own terms. If you stand still, or ignore her, she'll come right up and greet you. But she doesn't like being approached. "She has an internal

▲ Taylor, Julie McIntyre's Siamese cat, has the run of the grounds at Chanticleer, the spirited public pleasure garden in Wayne, Pennsylvania, where Julie is a resident fellow.

yardstick," Julie says, "and if you get too close, she runs away." Julie admits that Siamese, in her experience, are particularly demanding and intense. "The whole thing about cats being low-maintenance—I don't get it," she says. "Taylor wants somebody there all the time." Barbara Holland, in *Secrets of the Cat*, agrees; "Taking on a Siamese," she writes, "is rather like getting married."

Julie and Taylor have a daily routine. After she finishes her work in the office, they go for a walk around the garden. Taylor scampers off into the shrub and flower beds, flies down the sloping lawn, stops at the water garden for a drink, and every few minutes trots back to Julie, loudly meowing her pleasure. "We're in verbal contact all the time," Julie says.

Chanticleer is a delightful place for a daily walk. The thirty-one-acre property was preserved by the generosity of its original owners, the Rosengarten family, who endowed a foundation to maintain and develop the estate as a pleasure garden open to the public. Chris Woods, Chanticleer's chief horticulturist and executive director—who is partial to cats himself—has, with the help of eight full-time staff members, created a most pleasurable garden. Using the finest cultivars of trees, shrubs, and perennials that will flourish in the Pennsylvania countryside, he has established ravishing seasonal displays in the garden (in October, sweeps of golden amsonia by the entrance; a field of lavender blue *Aster tataricus* beyond the pond), as well as imaginative combinations of plants and sculpture. Tropical plants are staged near the entrance for a splashy welcome all summer. In winter, when the staff has extra time, they are encouraged to create fanciful garden furniture of their own design. A youthful air pervades the garden, a playfulness and a refreshing willingness to experiment.

Julia will be sad to leave when her fellowship ends. She is considering two jobs in conservation—one in Brooklyn, another in Hawaii. "I think Taylor would like Hawaii," she says.

▲ Chanticleer dazzles in its autumn dress with sweeps of amsonia turned golden yellow, old-fashioned pink chrysanthemums billowing out of the borders, and tall *Aster tataricus* painting an entire field lavender blue. Taylor, typically Siamese, likes to meow her pleasure to her mistress Julie as she explores the garden.

MONK-MONK among the FLOWERS

Tovah Martin is a prolific writer on gardens and gardening, and an expert on plants grown indoors and under glass. Her formative years were spent working at Logee's Greenhouses in Danielson, Connecticut, under the tutelage of her mother-in-law, Joy Logee Martin. In that jungly, magical world of passionflowers, scented geraniums, fragrant jasmines, bougainvilleas, and begonias, Tovah became an ardent and skilled gardener. And it was at Logee's, seven years ago, that she was presented with Monk-Monk.

A friend who worked for her in the greenhouses found the cat while he was out hunting with his dog. "They took a swim," Tovah recalls, "and there was this tiny kitten stuck

on a rock." Her friend brought the kitten to Tovah, who had just lost her eighteen-year-old cat. "It was as big as my hand," she says, "and weird looking, with a cowlick and triple paws." He would soon grow up to be a coon cat of enormous size, almost bigger than his diminutive mistress. "Everybody thought I'd adopted a bobcat," says Tovah.

Tovah named her coon kitten Maxwell, but within days he became known as Monk-Monk, she says, because "he's irascible," just like a monkey. "He's so conceited; he loves men and he's not at all interested in women. Well, we do sleep together," Tovah acknowledges, "but it's not what it could be." Monk-Monk, when he was featured on the cover of *Victoria* magazine, received stacks of fan mail. "And when I was at Logee's," Tovah says, "he got more Christmas cards than I did."

Tovah now lives in Roxbury, Connecticut, in an old converted barn where she writes her books and tends

▲ Monk-Monk, a foundling Maine coon cat adopted seven years ago by garden writer Tovah Martin, peers out from beneath a white-blooming bougainvillea in Tovah's Connecticut green-house.

▲ Dressed for winter weather in his Elizabethan ruff, Monk-Monk neverthe-less prefers to spend the cold months indoors, catch-ing rays of sunshine in the garden room off Tovah's converted barn.

her flowers, inside and out. Monk-Monk mostly sits on the porch in the summer, gazing out at Tovah's blowsy beds of perennials and annuals; he spends all winter lounging in the greenhouse, half hidden in the bougainvil-lea. "Maine coons always know how to dress," Tovah observes. "They shed a lot of their coat in summer, and then develop a really good Elizabethan ruff in winter. He's too handsome for words in his winter coat."

When the sun has deserted the greenhouse in winter, Monk-Monk drapes himself over the heat vents. "He doesn't love winter," she says. "He's not really a Maine coon cat. He's a Bermuda coon cat."

cattails

▶ clockwise *Lois Himes's twelve-year-old Felina waves her plume of a tail; Plucky Lucky, found under a bush, mauled and with a broken tail, lives a happy life now in the Cabots' splendid garden; Achilles hunts for frogs in the bog; Wink disappears down a bamboo-cloaked path; Abyssinian Isaac, still "fit as a fiddle" at age twenty, sharpens his claws in Larry Ashmead's Hudson River garden; Buckwheat and Barley head down a row of cornflowers.*